ENGLISH G

AF865555

access

1

WORKBOOK FÖRDERAUSGABE

Cornelsen

Here we go!

1 Read and write. Lies und schreib.

1 Hello!
My name is Silky.
What's your name?

2 My name is

______________________________ .

3 I'm 2 years old.
How old are you?

4 I'm ______________________________ years old.

5 I'm from Plymouth.
Where are you from?

6 I'm from ____________________________________ .

TIP
Deine Lernwörter findest du ab Seite 10.

2 Match the words and the pictures. Ordne die Wörter und Bilder zu.

castle

girl

river

pool

tower

hill

boy

boat

sea

big wheel

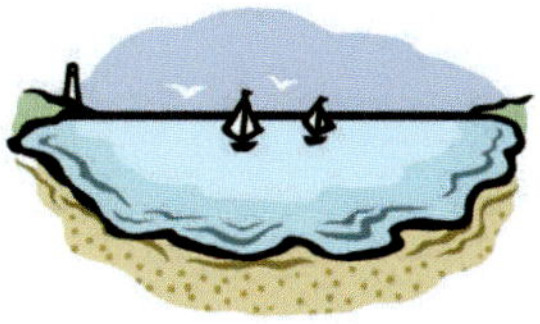

3 Find the 10 words from excercise 2. Finde die 10 Wörter aus Übung 2.

A	Z	B	O	A	T	T	C
V	G	I	R	L	P	C	P
N	W	G	D	F	O	A	S
T	O	W	E	R	O	S	E
B	H	H	Q	X	L	T	A
O	J	E	K	L	T	L	G
Y	P	E	R	I	V	E	R
H	I	L	L	C	S	N	Y

Ex. 3: Lernstärkere S können die Übung 2 abdecken, wenn sie in Übung 3 arbeiten.

4 Write the days of the week. Schreib die Wochentage auf.

Sunday | Tuesday | Friday | ~~Monday~~ | Wednesday | Thursday | Saturday

1 Monday

2 T

3 ______

4 ______

5 ______

6 ______

7 ______

My favourite day is

______ .

5 Write the days of the week. Schreib die Wochentage.

						↓							
6													
4													
1				M	O	N	D	A	Y				
3													
2													
5													

Ex. 4: Das Wort *favourite* müssen Sie erklären.
Ex. 5: Die Zahlen beziehen sich auf die Wochentage.Eine Vorlage finden die S in Übung 4.

6 Label the pictures. Beschrifte die Bilder.

ant • bird • cat • dog • elephant • frog • monkey • rabbit

a ______________________

a ______________________

an ______________________

a ______________________

a ______________________

a ______________________

an ______________________

a ______________________

7 Draw your favourite animal. Mal dein Lieblingstier.

8 Write the colours. Schreib die Farben.

red • blue • green • yellow • black • brown • grey • white • purple

1 ______ 2 ______ 3 ______

4 ______ 5 ______ 6 ______

7 ______ 8 ______ 9 ______

My favourite colour is

______ .

9 Colour the animals. Mal die Tiere aus.

The dog is red.

The monkey is green.

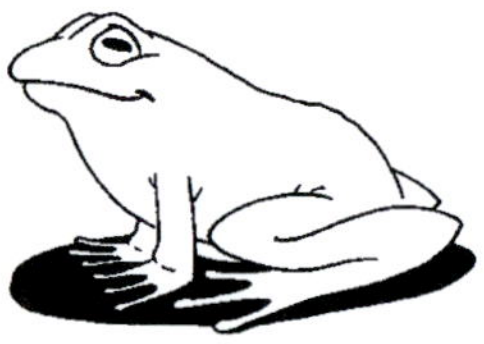

The frog is blue.

The cat is yellow.

Hier können Sie kleine mündliche Frage-Antwort-Übungen anschließen.
Ex. 8: Anschlussübung *What colour is this fish?*
Ex. 9: Anschlussübung *What colour is the dog?* usw.

10 Match the words and the pictures. Ordne die Wörter und Bilder zu.

exercise book

folder

pen

pencil

pencil case

rubber

school bag

glue stick

11 What's in your school bag? Was ist in deiner Schultasche?

a blue pencil

Ex. 10: Das Wort *folder* kommt im Schülerbuch nicht vor. Da viele Kinder mit Ordnern arbeiten, haben wir es hier aufgenommen.
Mündliche Anschlussübung nach Ex. 10: Sätze bilden nach dem Muster *The school bag is blue, red and yellow.*
Alternative: Fragen und Antworten *What colour is the school bag? – Blue.*

12 What's in the classroom? Was ist im Klassenzimmer?

door • ~~window~~ • board • desk • chair • poster • clock

1 window

2 ____________

3 ____________

4 ____________

5 ____________

6 ____________

7 ____________

13 Colour the picture. Mal das Bild oben aus.

The board is blue.
The door is yellow.
The clock is brown.
The chairs are red.

S können die Zeichnung weiter ausmalen.
Mündliche Anschlussübung: Sätze bilden nach dem Muster *The door is yellow.*
Alternative: Fragen und Antworten *What colour is the clock? – Brown.*

14 **Match the numbers and the words.** Ordne die Zahlen und Wörter zu.

11	one	8
6	two	12
9	three	1
3	four	4
10	five	7
5	six	2
	seven	
	eight	
	nine	
	ten	
	eleven	
	twelve	

I'm

_______________________________ .

My telephone number is

_______________________________ .

15 **How many fish?** Wie viele Fische?

[5] red fish	[ ] blue fish	[ ] green fish
[ ] yellow fish	[ ] orange fish	[ ] purple fish

Ex. 14: Für ihre eigene Telefonnummer müssen die S ggf. wissen, dass 0 *oh* ist.

S. 3	**Plymouth**		
	girl	Mädchen	
	boy	Junge	
	river	Fluss	
	sea	Meer	
	pool	Schwimmbad	
	boat	Boot	
	hill	Hügel	
	castle	Burg, Schloss	
	tower	Turm	
	big wheel	Riesenrad	

S. 4	**Days of the week**	**Wochentage**	
	Monday	Montag	
	Tuesday	Dienstag	
	Wednesday	Mittwoch	
	Thursday	Donnerstag	
	Friday	Freitag	
	Saturday	Samstag	
	Sunday	Sonntag	

S. 5	**Animals**	**Tiere**	
	ant	Ameise	
	bird	Vogel	
	cat	Katze	
	dog	Hund	
	elephant	Elefant	
	frog	Frosch	
	monkey	Affe	
	rabbit	Kaninchen	

S. 6	**Colours**	**Farben**	
	red	rot	
	yellow	gelb	
	blue	blau	
	green	grün	
	brown	braun	
	orange	orange	
	grey	grau	
	pink	pink	
	purple	lila	
	black	schwarz	
	white	weiß	

S. 7	**School things**	**Schulsachen**	
	school bag	Schultasche	
	pen	Stift	
	pencil	Bleistift	
	pencil case	Federmäppchen	
	rubber	Radiergummi	
	exercise book	Heft	
	folder	Ordner	
	glue stick	Klebestift	

Diese Seiten dienen als „Vokabelheft". Auf die Schreiblinie können die S das englische Wort schreiben.

New words

S. 8	**Classroom**	**Klassenzimmer**	
	desk	Schreibtisch	
	chair	Stuhl	
	board	Tafel	
	door	Tür	
	window	Fenster	
	poster	Poster	
	clock	Uhr	

S. 9	**Numbers**	**Zahlen**	
	one	eins	
	two	zwei	
	three	drei	
	four	vier	
	five	fünf	
	six	sechs	
	seven	sieben	
	eight	acht	
	nine	neun	
	ten	zehn	
	eleven	elf	
	twelve	zwölf	

S. 2	What's your name? My name is … .	Wie heißt du? Ich heiße … .
S. 2	How old are you? I'm … years old.	Wie alt bist du? Ich bin … Jahre alt.
S. 2	Where are you from? I'm from … .	Wo kommst du her? Ich bin aus … .
S. 4	What's your favourite day? My favourite day is … .	Was ist dein Lieblingstag? Mein Lieblingstag ist … .
S. 5	What's your favourite animal? My favourite animal is a(n) … .	Was ist dein Lieblingstier? Mein Lieblingstier ist ein(e) … .
S. 6	What's your favourite colour? My favourite colour is … .	Was ist deine Lieblingsfarbe? Meine Lieblingsfarbe ist … .
S. 9	What's your telephone number? My telephone number is … .	Wie ist deine Telefonnummer? Meine Telefonnummer ist … .

1 Unit

The first day at school

1 Write about the Plymouth kids. Schreib über die Plymouth Kinder.

Justin | Lucy | Sam

He's from • She's • She's at • He's • She's from • He's at

Maya

She's 11.

She's at Coombe Dean School.

She's from Plymouth.

____

____________ 11.

____________ Plymstock School.

____________ Plymouth.

____

He's 11.

He's at Plymstock School.

He's from London.

____

____________ 12.

____________ Plymstock School.

____________ Plymouth.

TIP
Deine Lernwörter findest du ab Seite 24.

2 Complete the sentences. Vervollständige die Sätze.

~~mum~~ • dad • sister • brother • favourite animal • best friend

My name is Lucy.
Lucy Pascoe.
And this is my family.

This is my
mum ____________.

And this is my
____________.

I have one
____________,
Holly. We live in Plymouth.

My ____________
____________ is a rabbit.

And this is Maya. She's my
____________.

This is Maya's
____________, Mukesh.

3 Write about your family. Schreib über deine Familie.

____

____

____

____

____

Ex. 3: Für Kinder, die keine Geschwister haben, müssten Sie ggf. einführen *I have no brothers or sisters*.

 **he**  **she** für Personen  **it** für Dinge

4 Complete the word spiders. Vervollständige die Wortspinnen.

clock • door • Maya • ~~Justin~~ • my brother • my dad • my mum • ~~chair~~ • my schoolbag • my sister • poster • Sam • window • ~~Lucy~~

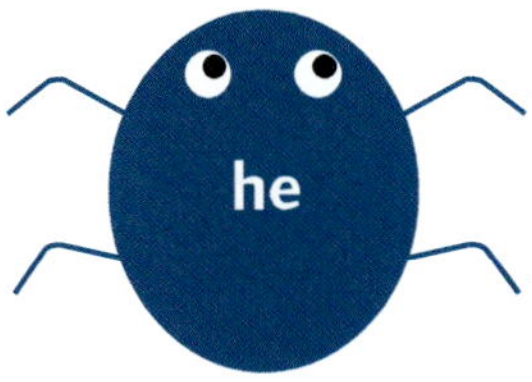

______ Justin
______ ______

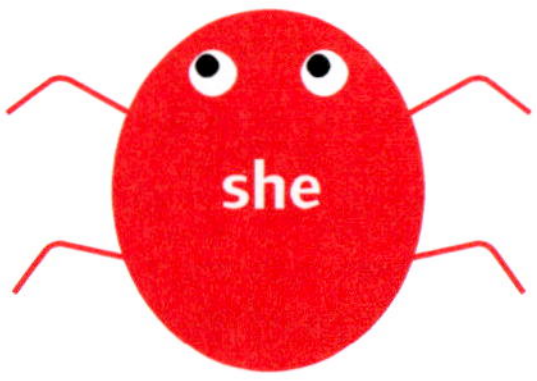

______ ______
Lucy ______

______ ______
______ chair
______ ______

5 Complete with *He's*, *She's* or *It's*. Vervollständige mit *He's*, *She's* oder *It's*.

1 Justin is at Plymstock. He's 12.

2 Holly is Lucy's sister. ______ at Plymstock too.

3 Plymstock is a school. ______ in Plymouth.

4 The Plymstock uniform is nice. ______ blue.

5 Mukesh is Maya's brother. ______ in Year 9.

6 Sam is from London. ______ in Year 7.

The pencil **is** green. It **isn't** red.

6 Complete with *is* or *isn't*. Vervollständige mit *is* oder *isn't*.

The clock **is** ________ red.	The clock **isn't** ________ red. It's green.
The boy ________ 4 years old.	The boy ________ 4 years old. He's 5 years old.
The dog ________ black and white.	The dog ________ black and white. It's brown and white.
The boy's sister ________ happy.	The boy's sister ________ happy. She's sad.

7 Complete with *is* or *isn't*. Vervollständige mit *is* oder *isn't*.

1 Sam **is** ________ from London.
2 Sam **isn't** ________ at Coombe Dean.
3 Lucy ________ at Plymstock.
4 Plymstock ________ in Germany.
5 Justin ________ 9 years old.
6 Maya ________ Lucy's friend.

8 Read Dan's email. Lies Dans E-Mail.

Hi!
My name is **Dan Miller**. I'm **12**. I'm from **Plymouth**.
I'm at **Plymstock School** in Year **8**. Sam is my friend, but he isn't in my class.
I have **a sister**, **Gemma**. She's at Plymstock too.
My favourite colour is **blue** and my favourite animal is **my dog Charlie**.
My favourite day is **Saturday**.
Bye! **Dan**

9 Right or wrong? Richtig oder falsch?

	Right	Wrong		Right	Wrong
1 Dan is 12.	✔	☐	2 Dan is in Year 12.	☐	☐
3 Gemma is Dan's sister.	☐	☐	4 Gemma is at Plymstock.	☐	☐
5 Dan is in Sam's class.	☐	☐	6 Dan's favourite day is Sunday.	☐	☐

10 Write Dan an email. Schreib Dan eine E-Mail.

Hi Dan!
____

My name is …
____

____

____

____

Ex. 10: Lernstärkere S können die Mail auch frei schreiben ohne der Vorlage genau zu folgen.

11 What time is it? Wie spät ist es?

It's 5 __________ o'clock.

It's __________ o'clock.

It's __________ o'clock.

It's __________ o'clock.

____

____

12 Answer the questions. Beantworte die Fragen.

Lesson	Monday	Tuesday	Wednesday	Thursday	Friday
9:00–10:00	Maths	PE	German	PE	Art
10:00–11:00	Music	Biology	Biology	English	Maths
Break 11:00–11:30					
11:30–12:30	English	Art	English	Maths	English
Lunch 12:30–2:00					
2:00–3:00	German	Music	German	Biology	PE

1 What time is maths on Monday? It's at 9 ________ o'clock.

2 What time is biology on Tuesday? It's at __________ o'clock.

3 What time is music on Tuesday? It's at __________ o'clock.

4 What time is German on Wednesday? It's at __________ o'clock and at __________ o'clock.

5 What time is English on Thursday? ____________________

6 What time is art on Friday? ____________________

Ex. 12: Wenn machbar, können und sollen die S natürlich auch halbe und Viertelstunden lernen. Für den Stundenplan nach Möglichkeit auch 11:30 als *eleven thirty* einführen. Anschlussübung: *Write your timetable in English*.

13 Write the months in the boxes. Schreib die Monate in die Kästchen.

November • May • ~~January~~ • September • July • March

January

February

April

June

August

October

December

Draw pictures
for April, July, October
and December.

> Wenn du etwas kannst, sagst du: **I can**.
> Wenn du etwas nicht kannst, sagst du: **I can't**.

14 Complete with *can* or *can't*. Vervollständige mit *can* oder *can't*.

Morph **can** write emails. I ______ write emails.

Morph **can't** read German books. I ______ read German books.

Morph ______ write a timetable. I ______ write a timetable.

Morph ______ play football. I ______ play football.

Morph ______ swim. I ______ swim.

Morph ______ speak English. I ______ speak English.

---

can lässt sich auch gut im Klassenzimmer üben: *What can you see? – I can see a board.* | *I can see a blue poster.* usw.

15 Read the story. Lies die Geschichte.

Chaos at the corner shop

corner shop kleiner Laden • **great** toll • **always** immer

16 Right or wrong? Richtig oder falsch?

	Right	Wrong
1 Maya is happy at Coombe Dean School.	✔	☐
2 Sam is Lily's big brother.	☐	☐
3 Maya is Sam's sister.	☐	☐
4 Sam is good at kung fu.	☐	☐
5 Maya isn't a good swimmer.	☐	☐
6 Sam is in the shop with his sister.	☐	☐

Am Ende der Unit finden Sie im Workbook jeweils eine gekürzte und vereinfachte Fassung des Unit-Texts aus dem SB.

S. 14	he	er	
	she	sie	
	he's	er ist	
	she's	sie ist	
	He's from … .	Er ist aus … .	
	She's from … .	Sie ist aus … .	

S. 15	**Family & friends**	**Familie & Freunde**	
	mum	Mama	
	dad	Papa	
	sister	Schwester	
	brother	Bruder	
	best friend	bester Freund/ beste Freundin	
	favourite animal	Lieblingstier	

S. 19	**Time**	**Uhrzeit**	
	10 o'clock	10 Uhr	
	11 o'clock	11 Uhr	
	12 o'clock	12 Uhr	

S. 19	**Timetable**	**Stundenplan**	
	art	Kunst	
	biology	Biologie	
	English	Englisch	
	German	Deutsch	
	maths	Mathe	
	music	Musik	
	PE	Sport	
	favourite subject	Lieblingsfach	

S. 20	**Months**	**Monate**	
	January	Januar	
	February	Februar	
	March	März	
	April	April	
	May	Mai	
	June	Juni	
	July	Juli	
	August	August	
	September	September	
	October	Oktober	
	November	November	
	December	Dezember	

S. 21	**Activities**	**Aktivitäten**	
	speak English	Englisch sprechen	
	write emails	E-Mails schreiben	
	read books	Bücher lesen	
	swim	schwimmen	
	play football	Fußball spielen	

S. 14	Lucy is at Plymstock School. She's from Plymouth. Sam is at Plymstock School. He's from London.	Lucy geht zur Plymstock School. She ist aus Plymouth. Sam geht zur Plymstock School. Er ist aus London.

S. 15	My name is … . This is my mum. This is my dad. I have one sister and one brother. We live in … . … is my best friend.	Mein Name ist … . Dies ist meine Mama. Dies ist mein Papa. Ich habe eine Schwester und einen Bruder. Wir wohnen in … . … ist mein bester Freund/ meine beste Freundin.

S. 16	This is my pencil. It's red. This is my bag. It's blue. This is my exercise book. It's green.	Dies ist mein Bleistift. Er ist rot. Dies ist meine Tasche. Sie ist blau. Dies ist mein Heft. Es ist grün.

S. 19	What time is it? It's 5 o'clock. What time is maths on Monday? At 9 o'clock. What's your favourite subject? My favourite subject is … .	Wie spät ist es? Es ist 5 Uhr. Wann ist Mathe am Montag? Um 9 Uhr. Was ist dein Lieblingsfach? Mein Lieblingsfach ist … .

My favourite subject is ____________________ .

S. 20	When's your birthday? My birthday is in June.	Wann hast du Geburtstag? Ich habe im Juni Geburtstag.

S. 21	I can speak English. I can't swim.	Ich kann Englisch sprechen. Ich kann nicht schwimmen.

My birthday is in August.
When's your birthday?

My birthday is in ______________________ .

Profile: Dan Miller

My name is Dan Milller. I'm 12 years old.
I'm from Plymouth in England.
My telephone number is 255361.
I have a sister. Her name is Gemma.
I have a dog too. His name is Charlie.
I'm at Plymstock School. I'm in Year 8.
My favourite subject at school is PE.
My favourite sport is football.
My birthday is in July.

Homes and families

1 Label the picture. Beschrifte das Bild.

Dan's bedroom • living room • bathroom • ~~Mum and Dad's bedroom~~ • kitchen • dining room

1 ______________________

2 Mum and Dad's bedroom

3 ______________________

4 ______________________

5 ______________________

6 ______________________

2 Read and write in your exercise book. Lies und schreib in dein Heft.

My house is in Plymouth.
We have two bedrooms, a living room, a dining room, a kitchen and a bathroom. And you?

My house/flat is in ______________________ .

We have … .

TIP

Deine Lernwörter findest du ab Seite 40.

Das Wort *flat* kommt im SB zu Beginn von Unit 1 vor (S. 18). Damit die S über ihr Zuhause sprechen können, ist es sinnvoll, es hier noch einmal in Erinnerung zu rufen.

3 What's in your bedroom? Was ist in deinem Zimmer?

books

TV

bed

chair

bed

____

____

____

____

____

desk

toilet

poster

lamp

pool

boat

4 Find the 10 words from exercise 3. Finde die 10 Wörter aus Übung 3.

T	D	B	E	D	C	A	C
V	T	F	G	X	P	Y	H
P	O	O	L	Q	O	T	A
R	I	U	B	J	S	K	I
P	L	B	O	A	T	L	R
D	E	S	K	Y	E	A	W
E	T	Z	F	L	R	M	N
B	O	O	K	S	P	P	D

Ex. 4: Lernstärkere S können Übung 3 ggf. abdecken, wenn sie Übung 4 machen.

5 Right or wrong? Richtig oder falsch?

	Right	Wrong
1 Dan's bedroom is big.	☑	☐
2 It's purple and pink.	☐	☐
3 His bed is near the window.	☐	☐
4 Dan's desk is blue.	☐	☐
5 His computer is on his bed.	☐	☐
6 You can see 5 posters in Dan's bedroom.	☐	☐

6 Write about your bedroom. Beschreib dein Zimmer.

My bedroom is big/small.

It's …

My bed is …

Ex. 5: Lernstärkere S können die falschen Sätze korrigieren und/oder weitere schreiben.

7 Complete the story. Vervollständige die Geschichte.

swim • go to bed • have breakfast • play • go to school • have dinner • ~~wake up~~

I wake up ______
at 6 o'clock.

I ______
at 7 o'clock.

Then YOU ______.

And I ______.

After lunch I ______
with my friends.

I ______
at 6 o'clock.

I ______
at 8 o'clock.

8 My day. Mein Tag.

______

______

______

______

______

Ex. 7: Diese Übung ist als Anschlussübung zu SB, S. 38 gedacht.

9 Match the sentences and the pictures. Ordne die Sätze und Bilder zu.

Abby's day

In the week Abby wakes up at 7 o'clock.

First she feeds her dog, Skip.

Then she has breakfast with her family.

She starts school at 9 o'clock.

She has lunch in the canteen.

After school she goes for a walk with Skip.

In the evening she watches TV with her family.

Before bed she texts her friends.

10 Correct the sentences. Korrigiere die Sätze.

Abby feeds Skip ~~after~~ breakfast. **No, she feeds Skip before breakfast.**

Abby has breakfast ~~with skip~~. ______________________

Abby has lunch ~~at home~~. ______________________

After school she goes for a walk with ~~Maya~~. ______________________

In the evening she ~~plays football~~ with her family. ______________________

11 Find the umbrella word. Finde den Oberbegriff.

numbers • days • animals • rooms

Monday
Wednesday
Saturday

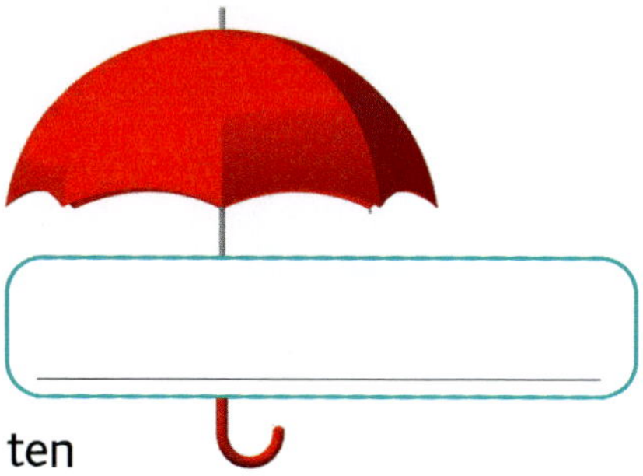

ten
three
five

kitchen
bathroom
bedroom

cat
rabbit
frog

12 Which word is different? Welches Wort ist anders?

1 March, ~~Saturday~~, May, July ____________________

2 pen, sister, pencil, folder ____________________

3 2 o'clock, 4 o'clock, 10 o'clock, music ____________________

4 mum, elephant, dad, brother ____________________

5 yellow, six, brown, grey ____________________

Ex. 11: S können unter den Oberbegriffen weitere Wörter aufschreiben.
Ex. 12: Auf die Schreiblinie können die S *the odd one out* schreiben und/oder das *umbrella word* für die 3 zusammengehörigen Wörter.

13 Complete Lucy's family tree. Vervollständige Lucys Stammbaum.

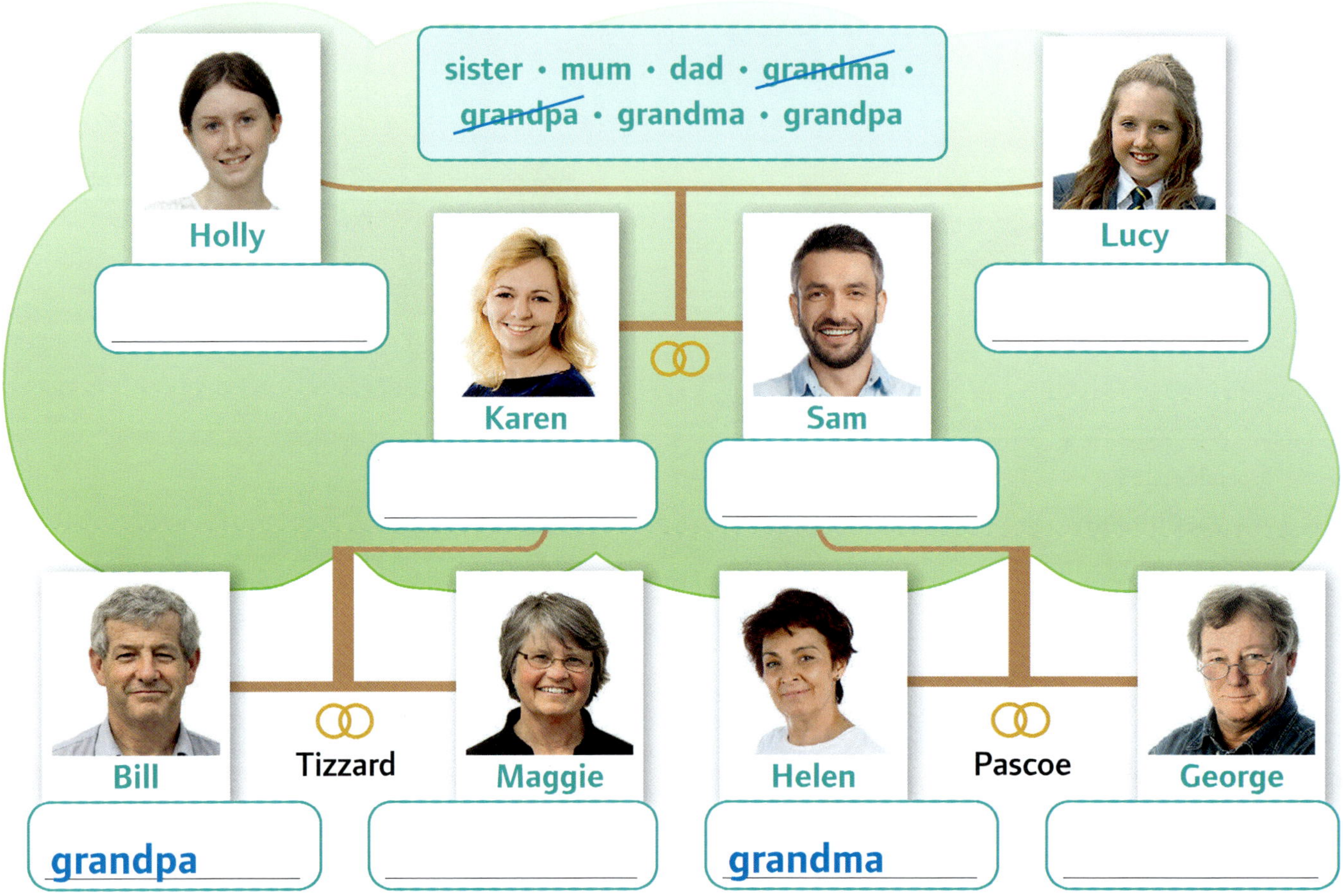

14 Right or wrong? Richtig oder falsch?

	Right	Wrong		Right	Wrong
1 Bill Tizzard is Lucy's grandpa.	✓	☐	2 George Pascoe is Lucy's dad.	☐	☐
3 Maggie Tizzard is Lucy's mum.	☐	☐	4 Holly is Lucy's brother.	☐	☐

15 Circle the right name. Kreis den richtigen Namen ein.

Lucy's mum:	Holly	(Karen)	Helen
Lucy's dad:	Sam	Bill	George
Lucy's sister:	Holly	Maggie	Helen
Lucy's grandma Tizzard:	Karen	Maggie	Helen
Lucy's grandma Pascoe:	Karen	Holly	Helen
Lucy's grandpa Tizzard:	Bill	Sam	George

16 Complete the phrases. Vervollständige die Ausdrücke.

go • go • meet • ~~play~~ • play • play • text • watch • watch

play ______ football	______ TV	______ to the park
______ computer games	______ DVDs	______ my friends
______ with my friends	______ to the shops	______ my friends

17 Complete Lucy's email. Vervollständige Lucys E-Mail.

go • meet • play • text • ~~wake up~~ • watch

Hi!
The weekend is great – no school! I **wake up** ______ late – at 10 o'clock.
After breakfast I do my homework. ☺

Then I ______ my best friend, Maya. In the afternoon, we ______

to the park or to the shops. In the evening, I ______ TV or ______

computer games. Before I go to bed, I often ______ my friends.
And you? Please write to me about your weekend.
Bye! Lucy

18 Write about your weekend. Schreib über dein Wochenende.

Hi Lucy! Thanks for your email. My weekend is great too. …

______

______

19 Sort the food and the drinks. Sortiere das Essen und die Getränke.

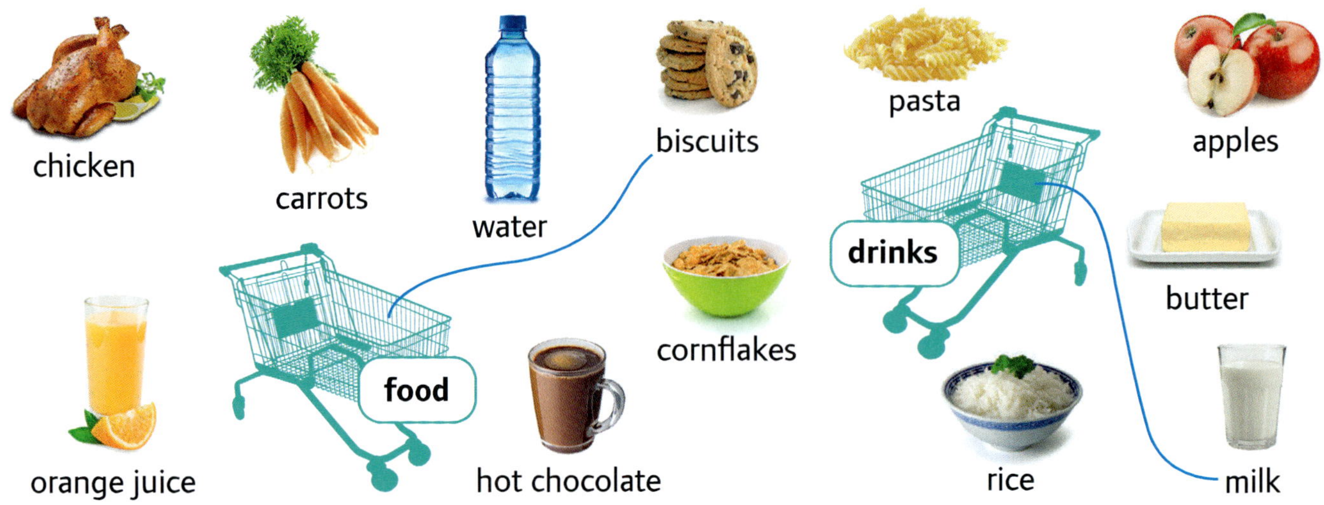

20 Complete the puzzle. Vervollständige das Rätsel.

bread • cheese • cream • fruit • jam • potatoes • soup • vegetables • yoghurt

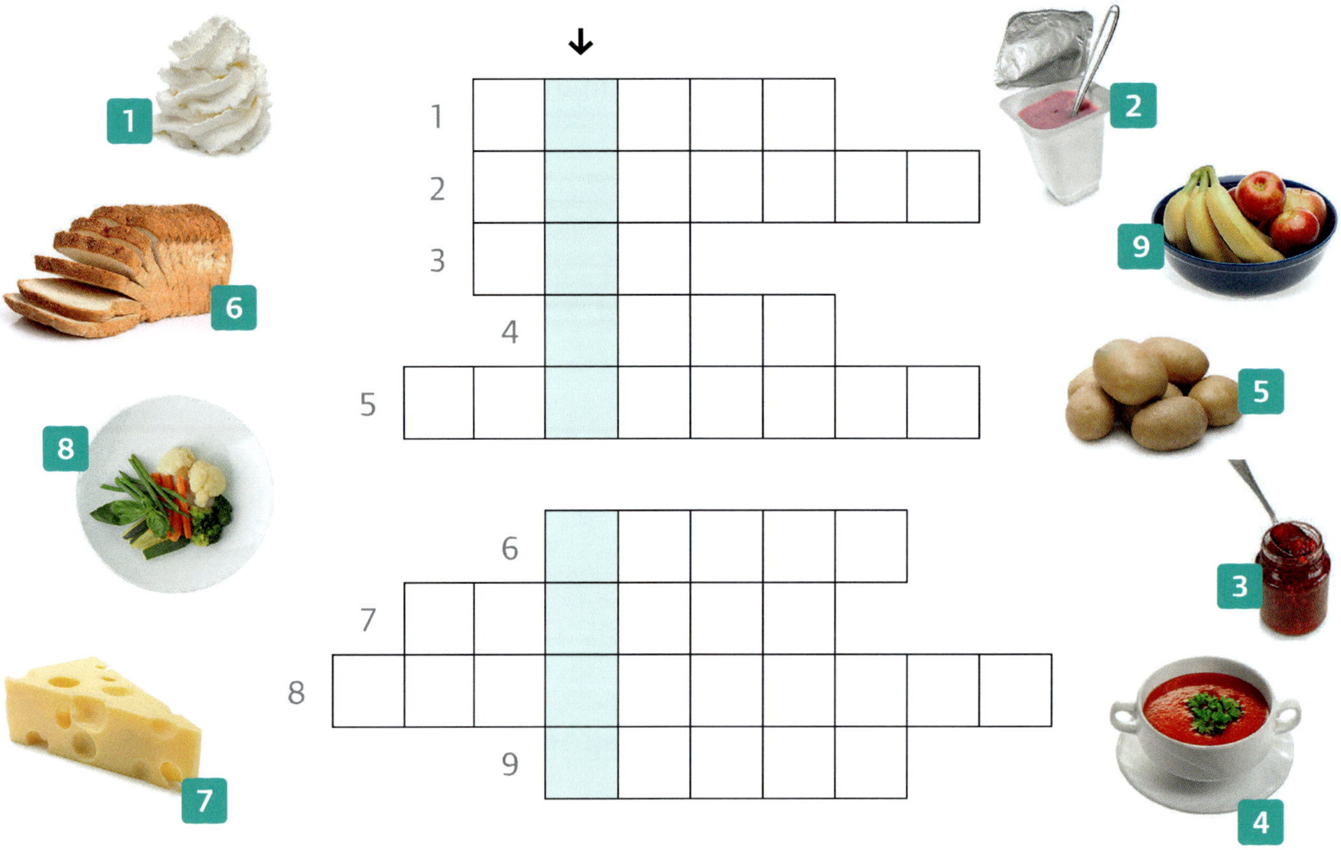

Sam's favourite food is _____ _____

21 Sort the words. Sortiere die Wörter.

bread • cheese • cornflakes • fruit • meat • milk • pizza • potatoes • sandwich • soup • spaghetti • toast • vegetables • water • yoghurt

breakfast	lunch	dinner
____________	____________	____________
____________	____________	____________
____________	____________	____________
____________	____________	____________
____________	____________	____________

I like fish,
but I don't like cornflakes.
And you?

I like ______________________________,

but I don't like ______________________________.

22 Write 3 sentences. Schreib 3 Sätze.

I like ______________________, but I don't like ______________________

____

____

Ex. 22: Die S können die Wörter von S. 36 verwenden. Weitere finden sich im SB in der Wordbank 5 auf S. 144/145.

23 Who says what? Wer sagt was?

Abby

Maya

Justin

Sam

Lucy

I have a little sister.
Her name is Lily.
I go to Plymstock School.
I'm 11.
I like kung fu.

I have no brothers or sisters.
My dad is in Boston.
I'm 12.
I go to Plymstock School.
I have a video camera.

I have a big brother.
His name is Mukesh.
I go to Coombe Dean.
I'm 11.
I like sailing.

I have a big sister.
Her name is Holly.
I'm 11.
I go to Plymstock School.
I like the animals on grandma's farm.

I have a brother, Tim.
I have a dog, Skip.
I'm 11.
I go to Plymstock School.
I like sailing.

Lernstärkere S können im Anschluss einen kurzen Text über sich oder über einen Freund/eine Freundin schreiben.

24 Read the story. Lies die Geschichte.

Saturday in Plymouth

1 It's Saturday. Justin and his mum are in Plymouth. Justin has a new video camera. It's a present from his dad in Boston.

Mum: Let's go to a café.
Justin: I don't like cafés. Can I go to the harbour, please?
Mum: OK. It's 3:45 now. Come to the café at 4:45. OK?
Justin: Thanks, Mum. Bye!

2 Justin is at the harbour now. He films seagulls, a boy and a girl and boats. The film is for his dad in Boston. He films a big sailing boat. Then he films an old boat. The name of the boat is *Blue Bird*. A small boy in a red T-shirt is on the boat.

3 It's 4:40. Time to go back to the café. Justin sees a woman with a police officer. A man is there too.

Woman: Please find my little boy, Tom.
Police officer: How old is Tom?
Man: He's 5. He can't swim.
Woman: He's in a red T-shirt and jeans. Please help!
Justin: I have a picture of a little boy on my video camera. Look!
Woman: That's Tom!
Police officer: Where's the boat?

4 Justin takes the police officer and Tom's mum and dad to the old boat. They find Tom. His mum is very happy.

5 Then Justin sees his mum. She's not happy. Justin is late! But the police officer is happy.

Police officer: Well done, Justin! Thank you for your help.

25 Match the pictures and the texts. Ordne die Bilder und Texte zu.

S. 28	**At home**	**Zu Hause**	
	house	Haus	
	flat	Wohnung	
	my bedroom	mein Zimmer	
	bathroom	Badezimmer	
	kitchen	Küche	
	living room	Wohnzimmer	
	dining room	Esszimmer	

S. 29	**My bedroom**	**Mein Zimmer**	
	bed	Bett	
	poster	Poster	
	chair	Stuhl	
	desk	Schreibtisch	
	lamp	Lampe	
	books	Bücher	
	TV	Fernseher	
	computer	Computer	
	sofa	Sofa	

S. 31 f.	**My day**	**Mein Tag**	
	wake up	aufwachen	
	have breakfast	frühstücken	
	go to school	zur Schule gehen	
	have lunch	zu Mittag essen	
	go home	nach Hause gehen	
	have dinner	zu Abend essen	
	go to bed	ins Bett gehen	

S. 34	**Family**	**Familie**	
	mum	Mama	
	dad	Papa	
	grandma	Oma	
	grandpa	Opa	
	sister	Schwester	
	brother	Bruder	

S. 35	**Activities**	**Aktivitäten**	
	play football	Fußball spielen	
	play computer games	Computerspiele spielen	
	play with my friends	mit meinen Freunden/ Freundinnen spielen	
	watch TV	fernsehen	
	watch DVDs	DVDs gucken	
	go to the shops	einkaufen gehen	
	go to the park	in den Park gehen	
	meet my friends	meine Freunde/ Freundinnen treffen	
	text my friends	meinen Freunden/ Freundinnen eine SMS schicken	

S. 36 f.	**Drinks**	**Getränke**	
	milk	Milch	
	water	Wasser	
	orange juice	Orangensaft	
	hot chocolate	Kakao	

S. 36 f.

Food	Essen
fruit	Obst
apple	Apfel
vegetables	Gemüse
carrots	Möhren
potatoes	Kartoffeln
meat	Fleisch
chicken	Hühnchen
fish	Fisch
soup	Suppe
pasta	Nudeln
spaghetti	Spagetti
rice	Reis
bread	Brot
toast	Toast
sandwich	belegtes Brot
biscuit	Keks
cornflakes	Cornflakes
jam	Marmelade
cheese	Käse
butter	Butter
yoghurt	Joghurt

Abby's day	My day
Abby wakes up at 7 o'clock.	I wake up at 7 o'clock too.
Abby has breakfast in the kitchen.	I have breakfast in the dining room.
Abby starts school at 9 o'clock.	I start school at 8 o'clock.
Abby has lunch in the canteen.	I have lunch at home.
After school Abby meets her friends.	After school I meet my friends.
In the evening Abby watches television.	In the evening I watch television too.
Abby goes to bed at 9 o'clock.	I go to bed at 8 o'clock.

Profile: Charlie

My name is Charlie. I'm 4 years old.
I live in Plymouth with Dan and his family.
I wake up at 6 o'clock.
I have breakfast in the kitchen.
After breakfast Dan and his sister go to school.
In the morning I play in the garden.
After lunch I go to the shops with Dan's mum.
In the afternoon I play football with Dan.
I have dinner at 7 o'clock.
My favourite food is meat. I like biscuits too!
In the evening we go to the park.
We play my favourite game – with a red ball.
My bed is in Dan's bedroom, under his bed. But I often sleep ON his bed! ☺

Clubs and hobbies

1 Label the clubs. Beschrifte die AGs.

Food Club • Art Club • Dance Club • ~~Book Club~~ • Football Team • Gardening Club

Book Club

- You like books?
- Come and talk about your favourite books.
- When: After school on Wednesday
- Where: In the library

- You like fruit and vegetables?
- Come and work in the school garden.
- When: After school on Friday
- Where: In the school garden

- For boys and girls in Years 7 and 8
- Make great party food or your favourite desserts.

- We meet in the canteen on Monday at 3:30.

Learn to make posters and cards.
Meet us in the art room on Tuesday at 3 o'clock.

Learn breakdance or hip-hop.
Meet us in the gym on Thursday at 4 o'clock.

- For boys and girls in Years 7 and 8
- Play football in a great team!
- We meet in the gym on Wednesday at 4:30.

TIP
Deine Lernwörter findest du ab Seite 57.

2 Right or wrong? Richtig oder falsch?

	Right	Wrong
1 You like books? The Book Club is for you!	☑	☐
2 The Gardening Club is in the library.	☐	☐
3 The Food Club is only for girls.	☐	☐
4 The Football Club is on Wednesday.	☐	☐
5 You can make a book in the Art Club.	☐	☐
6 You're a dance fan? The Dance Club is for you!	☐	☐

3 Make a poster for your club. Mach ein Poster für deine AG.

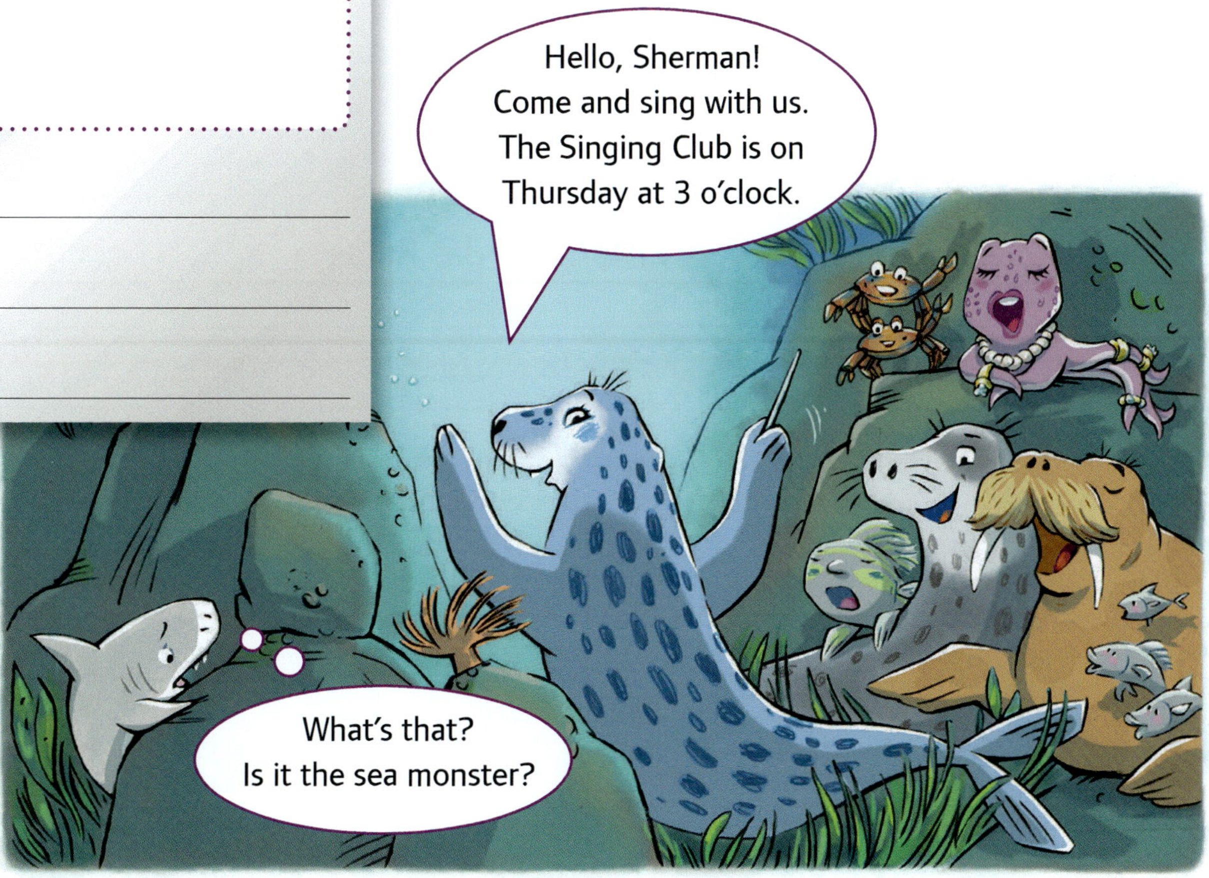

Das Poster gestalten die S für eine AG ihrer Wahl an der eigenen Schule.
Alternativ kann auch für Silkys Singing Club ein Poster gestaltet werden. Ideen dazu liefert die Illustration.

4 Label the pictures. Beschrifte die Bilder.

the guitar • gymnastics • ~~ice skating~~ • judo • skateboarding • swimming • table tennis • volleyball • yoga

go

go ice skating

play

do

5 Complete the puzzle. Vervollständige das Rätsel.

basketball • cards • drums • judo • piano • riding • skating • yoga

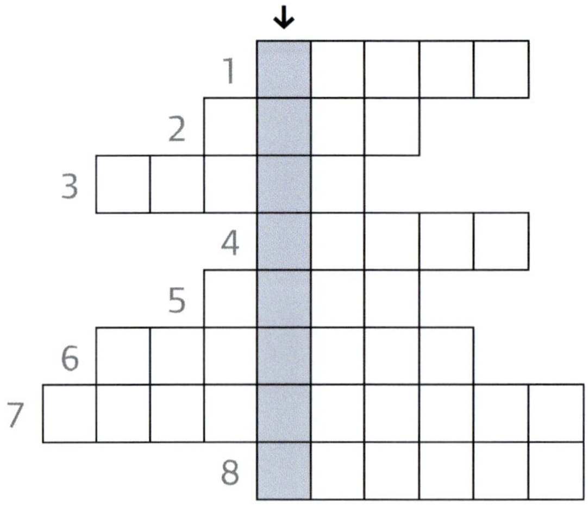

All kids like the ________ Club.

6 Complete the word spiders. Vervollständige die Wortspinnen.

~~judo~~ • ~~an instrument~~ • ~~skating~~ • basketball • computer games • football • homework • kung fu • sailing • swimming • tennis

go skating

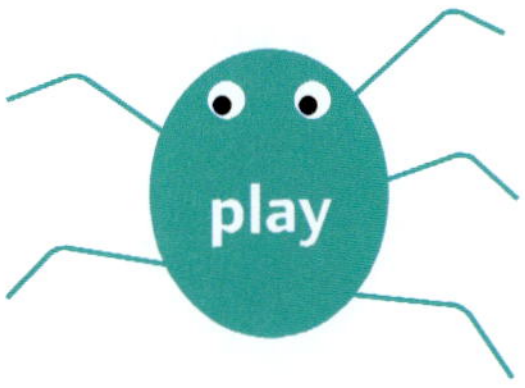

play an instrument

do judo

7 Complete what the kids say. Vervollständige, was die Kinder sagen.

do • don't do • go • don't go • go • don't go • ~~play~~ • ~~don't play~~ • play • don't play

Justin: I play computer games, but I don't play the guitar.

Sam: I ________ kung fu, but I ________ judo.

Maya: I ________ swimming, but I ________ riding.

Lucy: I ________ tennis, but I ________ football.

Abby: I ________ sailing, but I ________ skating.

And you? I ________, but I don't ________.

Ex. 7: Lernstärkere S können weitere Sätze über sich schreiben.

8 Make questions. Bilde Fragen.

~~books~~ • cats

Do you like books ____________________?

Do you ____________________?

football • computer games

Do you play ____________________?

____________________?

swimming • riding

Do you go ____________________?

____________________?

9 Questions and answers from exercise 8. Fragen und Antworten.

Do you like books?
Yes, I **do**.

Do you like cats?
No, I **don't**.

10 Fill in the question word. Setze das Fragewort ein.

How • What • When • ~~Where~~ • Where

1 Where ____________________ do you go to school, Dan? – I go to school in Plymouth.

2 ____________________ do you go to school? – I ride my bike.

3 ____________________ do you have lunch? – We have lunch in the canteen.

4 ____________________ do you do after school? – I meet my friends.

5 ____________________ do you do your homework? – I do my homework before dinner.

Ex. 8: Lernstärkere S können weitere Fragen formulieren.
Ex. 9: Als Vorlage für die Fragen und Antworten dient Übung 8.

11 Make questions. Bilde Fragen.

1 you / Where / live / do / ? Where do you live?

2 meet / your friends / do / you / When / ? ______

3 go / you / Where / do / to school / ? ______

4 have breakfast / When / you / do / ? ______

5 do / at weekends / do / you / What / ? ______

12 Complete Dan's email. Vervollständige Dans E-Mail.

What do you do at weekends? • Where do you go to school? • ~~Where do you live?~~ • What do you do after school? • Do you have a dog or a cat? • Do you have any brothers or sisters?

Hi!
My name is Dan. I'm your new friend. I live in Plymouth. Where do you live?

I have a sister, Gemma. ______

I go to Plymstock School in Plymouth. ______

After school I go to the park with my friends. ______

I have a dog, Charlie. ______

At weekends I meet my friends. We play football or computer games. ______

______

Please write!
Bye! Dan

Ex. 11: Im zweiten Schritt fragen sich S gegenseitig.
Ex. 12: Lernstärkere S können eine E-Mail mit ihren Antworten an Dan schreiben.

13 Read about Amira and Ranjiv. Lies über Amira und Ranjiv.

This is Amira. And this is her brother Ranjiv.
Amira is 11 and Ranjiv is 13.
Amira goes to Coombe Dean School.
Ranjiv goes to Coombe Dean too.
Amira likes maths, but she doesn't like English.
Ranjiv likes English, but he doesn't like maths.
Amira plays tennis on Saturday.
Ranjiv plays football on Sunday.
She plays the drums and he plays the guitar.
Amira has a rabbit, Hector. Ranjiv has a guinea pig, Honey.

Now complete the table. Jetzt vervollständige die Tabelle.

	age	school	likes	doesn't like	sports	hobbies	animals
Amira	___	___	___	___	___	___	___
Ranjiv	___	___	___	___	___	___	___

14 Abby and Tim. Write a text. Abby und Tim. Schreib einen Text.

	age	school	likes	doesn't like	sports	hobbies	animals
Abby	11	Plymstock	art	maths	sailing	hockey	dog, Skip
Tim	14	Plymstock	maths	art	skateboarding	piano	cat, Mink

This is Abby______. And this is her brother ______________.

Abby is 11 and Tim is _____. Abby goes to …______________________

____

Ex. 14 ist eine anspruchsvolle Aufgabe. Die Textvorlage für einen Text über Abby und Tim finden die S in Übung 13, die Informationen zu den beiden in der Tabelle. Den Text müssen die S in ihr Heft schreiben.

Does Silky like crabs?
Yes, she does.

Does Morph like gymnastics?
No, he doesn't.

15 Ask questions about Amira. Stell Fragen über Amira.

1 live in Plymouth / Amira / Does / ? **Does Amira live in Plymouth?**
– Yes, she does.

2 Does / go to Plymstock School / she / ? **Does she** ______
– No, she doesn't.

3 have a brother / Amira / Does / ? ______
– Yes, she does.

4 like maths / Does / Amira / ? ______
– Yes, she does.

5 she / play football / Does / ? ______
– No, she doesn't.

16 Ranjiv: Questions and answers. Ranjiv: Fragen und Antworten.

1 live in Plymouth / Ranjiv / Does / ? **Does Ranjiv live in Plymouth?**
– Yes, **he does**.

2 Does / go to Plymstock School / he / ? **Does he** ______

– No, ______.

3 like maths / Ranjiv / Does / ? ______

– No, ______.

4 play the drums / Does / Ranjiv / ? ______

– No, ______.

5 he / have a guinea pig / Does / ? ______

– Yes, ______.

Ex. 15 und 16: Lernstärkere S können weitere Fragen und Antworten bilden.

17 Find and colour the pairs. Finde und male die Gegensatzpaare aus.

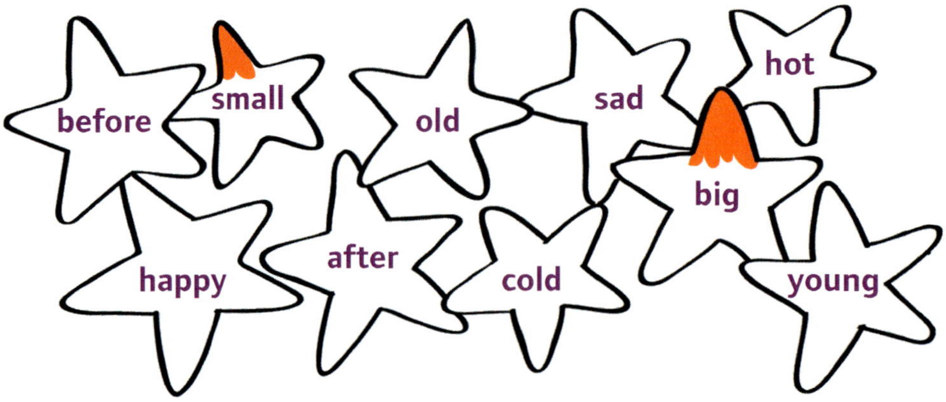

18 Put in the words from the stars. Setze die Sternwörter ein.

1 Silky is **happy** because she has friends. Morph is **sad** because he doesn't have any friends.

2 In winter it's ____________ and in summer it's ____________.

3 Abby feeds Skip ____________ breakfast. She goes to school ____________ breakfast.

4 Abby's house is ____________, but her bedroom is ____________.

5 My little sister is ____________ and my grandma is ____________.

19 Complete with *and, because* or *but*. Vervollständige die Sätze.

1 I want a drink **because** I'm thirsty.

2 Justin can't meet Sam ____________ he has no time.

3 I play football ____________ I do kung fu.

4 Sam has a sister ____________ he doesn't have a brother.

5 Maya is Lucy's friend ____________ she's Abby's friend too.

6 Lucy has two grandmas ____________ she has two grandpas.

7 Dan has a dog ____________ he doesn't have a cat.

8 Justin skypes with his dad ____________ he's in Boston.

20 small or BIG letters? kleine oder GROẞE Buchstaben?

n N   m M   l L   p P

My **n**ame is **M**orph. I live in the ____ibrary at ____lymstock School.

p P   t T   e E

It's in ____lymouth, a big ____own in ____ngland.

e E   g G

You can learn ____nglish at my school. I can't speak ____erman.

m M

There are lots of clubs at ____y school.

w W   m M   f F

I'm in the Reading Club. ____e meet on ____onday and on ____riday.

21 Answer the questions. Beantworte die Fragen.

Come to Dartmoor Zoo!

See your favourite animals!
Visit our lions, tigers, giraffes, bears, monkeys and snakes.
Watch them feed!

Visit the *Safari Café* for lunch, sandwiches, ice cream and hot and cold drinks.

Kids can have fun in the kids' play areas!
Sorry, no dogs!

Opening times
Open every day 10 am – 6 pm

Prices

Adults	£10.95
Children 5–15 years	£8.95
Family tickets	£35.00

1 Was gibt es dort zu sehen?
2 Wie sind die Öffnungszeiten?
3 Was kosten die Tickets für Kinder?
4 Kann man dort auch was essen?
5 Und kann man auch was trinken?
6 Können wir den Hund mitnehmen?

Ex. 20: Lernstärkere S können einen ähnlichen Text über sich selbst schreiben.
Ex. 21 ist als Mediation-Aufgabe gedacht. Deshalb können die Antworten auf Deutsch gegeben werden.

22 Read the story. Lies die Geschichte.

The captain's ghost

A great story

Lucy has a dream. She tells Sam and Maya. They think Lucy's dream is a great story for a film. They want to tell Justin and Abby their idea. Lucy's dream is about two girls, Abigail and May, and Abigail's dog, Skipper.

1 Skipper finds an old book

Abigail and her friend May are at Abigail's house. Abigail has a dog, Skipper. The two girls and the dog go to the attic. Skipper finds an old book. There is a name and a date on the book: *Captain Justin Pascoe, 1581*.

May: 1581. This book is very old!

Abigail: Look – there's an address too: *New Street, Plymouth*. And what's this?

May: A map of a house. On the map you can see where Captain Pascoe has his gold.

Abigail: Gold!

2 Abigail finds a letter

Abigail finds a letter in the book.
She reads the letter.

10th February 1581
Dear Father,
Mother is very sick. We don't have any money.
We can't eat. Please come home.
Please help us.
Lucille

3 ______

Skipper finds a bottle. Abigail opens it. It smells strange.

Abigail: I'm very tired.

May: I'm very tired too.

4 ______

Abigail and May wake up. They run out of the house with Skipper. Where are they? They meet a boy.

Abigail: Hello. My name is Abigail. This is May.

Samuel: Hello. I'm Samuel.

Abigail: Where are we?

Samuel: In Plymouth.

May: What year is it?

Samuel: 1581.

Abigail: The year of the book.

May: We want to find Lucille Pascoe. We want to help her.

Samuel: Lucille is my friend. This is her house.

5 ______

Samuel: Hello Lucille.

Lucille: Hello Samuel.

Samuel: May and Abigail can help you.

Lucille: Hello May, hello Abigail.

May: We have your father's book.

Lucille: But my father is dead. You can't help me. Please go.

Abigail: We have a map too. On the map you can see where your father's gold is.

6

A door opens. Skipper starts barking – woof, woof, woof. It's a ghost!

Ghost: Stop! The girls have my book.
Lucille: Father! Abigail and May are friends. They want to help.
Skipper: Woof, woof, woof!
Ghost: How can they help?
May: We have a map. The map shows where your gold is. Lucille, please take the map. It's for you.
Lucille: Father, we can find your gold. Father? But the ghost isn't there.

7

The children and the dog go to the attic. Samuel finds a small door. Lucille opens the door.

Lucille: Gold! The gold is here!
May: The gold is for you and your mother, Lucille.
Lucille: This gold coin is for you, May.
May: Thank you.
Samuel: I'm thirsty. Can I have a drink, please?
Lucille: Yes, let's go to the kitchen. I can make some tea.

8

May: This tea is strange.
Abigail: I'm very tired.
May: I'm very tired too.
Skipper: Woof, woof.
Abigail: Wake up, May.
May: Where are we?
Abigail: At home. What's that in your hand, May?
May: A gold coin.

dream Traum • **tell** erzählen • **attic** Dachboden • **map** (Land-)Karte • **sick** krank • **bottle** Flasche • **it smells strange** es riecht komisch • **tired** müde • **dead** tot • **ghost** Geist • **coin** Münze

23 Put in the headings. Füge die Überschriften ein.

The end of Lucy's dream • Skipper finds a bottle • Abigail and May meet Lucille • ~~Skipper finds an old book~~ • The gold • The ghost • Plymouth in 1581 • ~~Abigail finds a letter~~

24 Put in the names. Setze die Namen ein.

~~Abigail~~ • Abigail • ~~May~~ • May • Lucy • Skipper • Samuel • Lucille • Lucille • Lucille • Captain Pascoe • Captain Pascoe

1 May and Abigail go to the attic.

2 ______________ finds a book.

3 ______________ is the name in the book.

4 May and ______________ meet a boy. His name is ______________.

5 ______________ is Samuel's friend.

6 May and Abigail want to help ______________.

7 The ghost is ______________.

8 ______________ finds her father's gold.

9 Lucille gives ______________ a gold coin.

10 The ghost story is ______________'s dream.

25 Who's who in the film? Match. Wer ist wer im Film? Ordne zu.

Justin thinks Lucy's dream is a great idea for a film. But who's who?

Sam

Maya

Lucy

Skip

Abby

Abigail **Lucille** **Samuel** **Skipper** **May**

S. 44 f.	**Clubs**	**AGs (Arbeitsgemeinschaften)**	
	Food Club	Koch-AG	
	Art Club	Kunst-AG	
	Dance Club	Tanz-AG	
	Book Club	Literatur-AG	
	Football Team	Fußball-Team	
	Gardening Club	Garten-AG	
	Singing Club	Gesangs-AG	
	Computer Club	Computer-AG	

S. 46	**Activities**	**Aktivitäten**	
	go ice skating	Schlittschuhlaufen	
	go skateboarding	Skateboard fahren	
	go swimming	schwimmen gehen	
	go riding	reiten gehen	
	go skating	Inliner fahren	
	play volleyball	Volleyball spielen	
	play table tennis	Tischtennis spielen	
	play football	Fußball spielen	
	play tennis	Tennis spielen	
	play hockey	Hockey spielen	
	play cards	Karten spielen	
	play computer games	Computerspiele machen	
	play an instrument	Instrument spielen	
	play the guitar	Gitarre spielen	
	play the piano	Klavier spielen	
	do gymnastics	turnen	
	do judo	Judo machen	
	do yoga	Yoga machen	
	do homework	Hausaufgaben machen	

S. 48	**Question words**	**Fragewörter**	
	how	wie	
	what	was	
	when	wann	
	where	wo	
	why	warum	

S. 52	**Opposites**	**Gegensätze**	
	after – before	nach – vor	
	big – small	groß – klein	
	happy – sad	glücklich – traurig	
	young – old	jung – alt	
	hot – cold	heiß – kalt	

S. 52	**Linking words**	**Verbindungswörter**	
	and	und	
	but	aber	
	because	weil	

Circle the sentences for you. Kreise die Sätze für dich ein.

1 I play computer games. I don't play computer games.

2 I go swimming. I don't go swimming.

3 I go riding. I don't go riding.

4 I play an instrument. I don't play an instrument.

5 I do my homework. I don't do my homework.

Asking questions. Fragen stellen.

Du willst herausfinden, wo jemand wohnt:
Where do you live?

Du willst herausfinden, wo jemand zur Schule geht:
Where do you go to school?

Du willst herausfinden, wie jemand zur Schule geht:
How do you go to school?

Du willst herausfinden, was jemand nach der Schule macht:
What do you do after school?

Du willst herausfinden, was jemand am Wochenende macht:
What do you do at the weekend?

Du willst herausfinden, wann jemand seine Freunde trifft:
When do you meet your friends?

Du willst herausfinden, ob jemand etwas mag:
Do you like ...?

Du willst herausfinden, ob jemand Geschwister hat:
Do you have any brothers or sisters?

Du willst herausfinden, ob jemand einen Hund oder eine Katze hat:
Do you have a dog or a cat?

4 Unit

Weekends

1 What do you do at the weekend? Was machst du am Wochenende?

	always	sometimes	never
Do you go to the cinema?	☐	☐	☐
Do you clean your bedroom?	☐	☐	☐
Do you do your homework?	☐	☐	☐
Do you watch TV?	☐	☐	☐
Do you play computer games?	☐	☐	☐
Do you meet your friends?	☐	☐	☐

2 Complete the sentences. Vervollständige die Sätze.

I always ______________________________

I sometimes ______________________________

3 Find 8 words. Finde 8 Wörter.

café • cinema • club • gym • ~~library~~ • museum • park • zoo

C	L	I	B	R	A	R	Y	P
A	S	M	U	S	E	U	M	A
F	Z	H	L	X	K	E	O	R
É	O	C	L	U	B	P	P	K
I	O	N	G	G	Y	M	B	M
A	L	C	I	N	E	M	A	L

TIP
Deine Lernwörter findest du ab Seite 70.

4 Complete the sentences. Vervollständige die Sätze.

Dan

Nina

Leo

at the zoo

at the gym

at the pool

Last Saturday Dan **was at the gym** ______.

Last Sunday Nina ______.

Last weekend Leo ______.

Tim + Abby

Justin + Sam

Lucy + Maya

at the shopping mall

at home

at the cinema

Last Saturday Tim and Abby **were at home** ______.

Last Sunday Justin and Sam ______.

Last weekend Lucy and Maya ______.

Mit den Fotos lassen sich sehr gut auch Fragen und Antworten üben:
Where was Dan? | *Were Lucy and Maya at home?* usw.

5 Circle the 12 verbs. Kreise die 12 Verben ein.

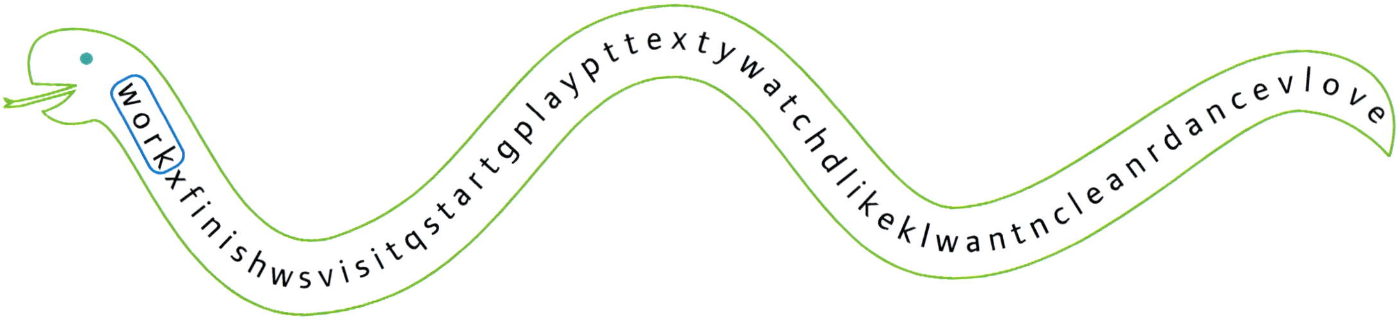

Write 4 verbs in the simple past. Schreib 4 Vergangenheitsformen.

work > worked ____________ ____________

____________ ____________

6 Complete in the simple past. Vervollständige in der Vergangenheit.

~~play~~ • visit • want • work

1 Last Saturday Sam played ____________ basketball.

2 Last weekend Justin's dad ____________ at the studios in Boston.

3 Last Sunday Holly ____________ her grandparents at the farm.

4 Yesterday Lucy ____________ to meet Maya, but Maya was with Abby.

7 Write the simple past forms. Schreib die Vergangenheitsformen.

ate • ~~came~~ • drank • had • made • went • won

come	came
drink	____________

eat	____________
go	____________

have	____________
make	____________
win	____________

8 Complete Nina's diary. Vervollständige Ninas Tagebuch.

boys • cake • CDs • dog • football • ~~party~~ • quiz • video

Dear Diary, 5th April

Last Saturday we had a fantastic

party ______. It was in Dan's garden.

I made pizza, Charlotte made a lot of sandwiches

and Emily made a chocolate ______.
It was very nice. And Dan's biscuits were great too. The party started at 3 o'clock and finished at 9 o'clock.

Five girls and five ______ came to

the party – and one ______, Charlie!

First we played ______ with Charlie.

Then we were hungry, so we had some cake and biscuits – Charlie too!

Later we had a music ______.
The girls won! After the quiz, we ate the pizza and sandwiches – they were great! And we drank lemonade. In the evening we

played some cool ______ and danced. Charlie loved the music!

We made a ______ of the party.
Charlie was the star!

After the party, we cleaned the kitchen.
Then I went home.

9 Correct the sentences. Korrigiere die Sätze.

1 The kids had a party on ~~Friday~~. The kids had a party on Saturday.

2 Nina made ~~sandwiches~~. ______

3 ~~Ten dogs~~ came to the party. ______

4 The ~~boys~~ won the quiz. ______

5 The kids ate the cake ~~after~~ the quiz. ______

6 They drank ~~milk~~. ______

7 After the party Nina went ~~to school~~. ______

Nach Übung 7 sicherstellen, dass die Bedeutung der Verben klar ist. Die Sätze in Übung 9 beziehen sich auf den Tagebucheintrag in Übung 8.

Wenn du gestern z. B. Fußball gespielt hast, sagst du:
I **played** football yesterday.

Wenn du gestern nicht Klavier gespielt hast, sagst du:
I **didn't play** the piano yesterday.

10 Complete in the simple past. Vervollständige in der Vergangenheit.

Morph's weekend was good!

- learn maths ✔
- clean shoes ✔
- play cards ✔
- finish book ✔

Morph learned ______ maths.

He ______ his shoes.

He ______ cards.

He ______ his book.

11 Complete in the simple past. Vervollständige in der Vergangenheit.

Sam's weekend was good too!

- learn maths
- clean shoes
- play with Lily
- finish book

1 He didn't learn ______ maths.

3 He ______ his shoes.

2 He ______ with Lily.

4 He ______ his book.

Ex. 10 und 11: Lernstärkere S können ein paar Sätze über ihr eigenes Wochenende schreiben: was sie gemacht und nicht gemacht haben.

12 Write the simple past forms. Schreib die Vergangenheitsformen.

~~did~~ • had • made • met • saw • went • won

~~didn't do~~ • didn't have • didn't make • didn't meet • didn't see • didn't go • didn't win

do	did	didn't do
go	___	___
have	___	___
make	___	___
meet	___	___
see	___	___
win	___	___

13 Put in the verbs from ex. 12. Setze die Verben aus Übung 12 ein.

1 Silky had crabs for dinner yesterday. Justin didn't have crabs for dinner.

2 Maya went to school yesterday. Lucy ___ to school – she was sick.

3 Maya met Abby after school. She ___ Lucy.

4 Justin did his maths homework. He ___ his English homework.

5 Sam saw Justin last weekend. He ___ Lucy and Maya.

6 Sam's mum made biscuits. She ___ a cake.

7 The girls won the quiz. The boys ___ the quiz.

14 Complete Lucy's diary. Vervollständige Lucys Tagebuch.

- didn't have • met • ~~was~~
- came • missed • was
- didn't like • was • went
- didn't eat • had • were
- was • went • were

Dear Diary May 4th

Today was my birthday. I ____________ a party at home. I ____________ my friends at the Hoe. Abby ____________ too. She ____________ late because she ____________ the bus. We ____________ on the Wheel. It ____________ great, but Sam ____________ the ride. After the ride we ____________ a picnic – the sandwiches and cake ____________ yummy. ☺ But Sam ____________ much. We ____________ home at 7 o'clock. It ____________ a great day and we ____________ all tired in the evening.

15 Right or wrong? Richtig oder falsch?

	Right	Wrong		Right	Wrong
1 Lucy had a party at home.	☐	☑	2 Abby didn't come.	☐	☐
3 All the kids liked the Wheel.	☐	☐	4 They had a great picnic.	☐	☐
5 Sam ate lots of food.	☐	☐	6 Lucy had a good birthday.	☐	☐

16 Answer the questions. Beantworte die Fragen.

Feeding times at Dartmoor Zoo

Our zoo is open all year.
In summer you can visit us from 10 am to 6 pm,
in winter from 10 am to 4 pm.

The animals usually feed at the same time every day.
Come and watch them!

10:00 Bears' morning feeding time
Watch the bears and learn lots of interesting information!

12:30 Monkeys' feeding time
Have fun and watch the monkeys eat their lunch. They love bananas!

12:30 Big cats' feeding time
Come and meet the lions – Solomen and Josie and the tigers – Vlad, Blotch and Stripe. These animals are always hungry!

15:30 Snakes' feeding time
Only 30 people (adults and kids) can watch. Don't come late! Listen to an interesting talk.

1 Macht der Zoo im Sommer um 16 Uhr zu? ______________________

2 Wie heißen die Tiere auf den Fotos auf Englisch? ______________________

3 Welche Tiere werden zuerst gefüttert? ______________________

4 Können wir allen Tieren bei der Fütterung zuschauen? ______________________

5 Was mögen die Affen? ______________________

6 Wie heißen die Tiger? ______________________

7 Gibt es auch nachmittags eine Fütterung? ______________________

Ex. 16 ist als Mediation-Aufgabe gedacht. Deshalb können die Antworten auf Deutsch gegeben werden.

17 Read the story. Lies die Geschichte.

A baby seal

15 October: on a beach on Ivy Island
A mother seal and her baby were on the sand near a pool. The baby was hungry. She drank her mother's milk. It was good. Soon the baby seal fell asleep in the warm sun. When she woke up, she was hungry again. Her mother wasn't there. Where was she? The baby seal was sad and hungry. She was tired, too tired to swim, too tired to play with the other baby seals in the pool.

18 October: in a boat near Ivy Island
Three children were in a boat – Abby and her two brothers Will and Tim. Abby was 9 years old. Will was the captain of the sailing boat.
Abby: I want to sail the boat.
Tim: No. You're only 9.
Abby: That's not fair. I can sail.
Will: You're too young, Abby.
Abby: Look! What's that on the beach? Stop!
Will: We can't stop.
Abby: But I can see an animal.
Tim: It isn't an animal. It's a rock.
Abby: No, it's a baby seal. Please stop.
Will: OK. Let's go to the beach.

10 minutes later: on the beach
Abby: It *is* a baby seal. We must help her.
Tim: Don't go near the seal. Seals can bite.
Abby: But she's sick. Where's her mother? Will, call the rescue centre.
Will: OK.

20 minutes later: on the beach
Abby: Look! I can see a boat with two men and a woman.
Tim: It's the rescue team.
Woman: Hello. We're from the rescue centre.
Abby: Hello. Please help. The baby seal is sick.
Man 1: Yes, and she's very hungry.
Abby: Where's her mother?
Man 2: Yesterday we found a dead seal near here – I think it was her mother.
Abby: That isn't fair.
Woman: No, it isn't fair. But you found her baby and we can help her.
Man 1: Yes, you found the baby seal, so you can give her a name.
Abby: What's a good name for a baby seal? I know – Silky. Her name is Silky.

seal Seerobbe · **beach** Strand · **hungry** hungrig · **sad** traurig · **tired** müde · **rock** Felsen · **bite** beißen · **rescue centre** Rettungsstation · **dead** tot

18 Find the right ending. Finde das richtige Satzende.

1 The baby seal	were in a boat.
2 Her mother	to the island.
3 Abby and her two brothers	was hungry.
4 Abby saw	a name, Silky.
5 The children sailed	the baby seal on the island.
6 Will called	came to help.
7 Three people from the rescue centre	wasn't there.
8 Abby gave the baby seal	the rescue centre.

19 Correct the sentences. Korrigiere die Sätze.

didn't call • didn't give • didn't help • ~~didn't play~~ • didn't sail • didn't see

1 The baby seal ~~played~~ with the other baby seals.

The baby seal didn't play with the other baby seals.

2 Abby ~~sailed~~ the boat. ____________________

3 Abby ~~saw~~ the mother seal. ____________________

4 Will ~~called~~ his father. ____________________

5 The rescue team ~~helped~~ the children. ____________________

6 The rescue team ~~gave~~ the baby seal a name. ____________________

Ex. 19: Lernstärkere S können Informationen aus dem Text ergänzen, z. B. *The baby seal didn't play with the other baby seals because she was tired.*

S. 60	**Weekend activities**	**Wochenendaktivitäten**	
	go to the cinema	ins Kino gehen	
	visit your grandparents	deine Großeltern besuchen	
	do your homework	Hausaufgaben machen	
	watch TV	fernsehen	
	play computer games	Computerspiele spielen	
	meet your friends	deine Freunde treffen	
	clean your bedroom	dein Zimmer sauber machen	
S. 63	have a party	ein Fest feiern	
	make pizza	Pizza machen	
	make sandwiches	belegte Brote machen	
	make a cake	einen Kuchen backen	
	have a quiz	ein Quiz machen	
	play music	Musik spielen	
	dance	tanzen	
	make a video	ein Video machen	
	go home	nach Hause gehen	

S. 60 f.	**Places**	**Orte**	
	at the zoo	im Zoo	
	at the gym	in der Turnhalle	
	at the café	im Café	
	at the library	in der Bücherei	
	at the museum	im Museum	
	at the park	im Park	
	at the pool	im Schwimmbad	
	at the shopping mall	im Einkaufszentrum	
	at home	zu Hause	
	at the cinema	im Kino	

S. 60	**How often?**	**Wie oft?**	
	always	immer	
	sometimes	manchmal	
	never	nie	

S. 61	**was**		
	I was	ich war	
	Dan was	Dan war	
	he was	er war	
	Lucy was	Lucy war	
	she was	sie war	

S. 61	**were**		
	you were	du warst	
	we were	wir waren	
	Lucy and Maya were	Lucy und Maya waren	
	they were	sie waren	

S. 61 f.	**Times**	**Zeiten**	
	last weekend	letztes Wochenende	
	last Saturday	letzten Samstag	
	last Sunday	letzten Sonntag	
	yesterday	gestern	

S. 62 f.	**Verbs**	**Verben**
	I work – I worked	ich arbeite – ich habe gearbeitet
	I learn – I learned	ich lerne – ich habe gelernt
	I play – I played	ich spiele – ich habe gespielt
	I visit – I visited	ich besuche – ich habe besucht
	I ask – I asked	ich frage – ich habe gefragt
	I text – I texted	ich schicke eine SMS – ich habe eine SMS geschickt
	I call – I called	ich rufe an – ich habe angerufen
	I watch TV – I watched TV	ich sehe fern – ich habe ferngesehen
	I like – I liked	ich mag – ich mochte
	I love – I loved	ich liebe – ich liebte
	I want – I wanted	ich will – ich wollte
	I start – I started	ich fange an – ich habe angefangen
	I finish – I finished	ich mache … fertig – ich habe … fertiggemacht
	I dance – I danced	ich tanze – ich habe getanzt
	I clean – I cleaned	ich mache sauber – ich habe saubergemacht

S. 63 f.	**More verbs**	**Weitere Verben**
	I eat – I ate	ich esse – ich habe gegessen
	I drink – I drank	ich trinke – ich habe getrunken
	I have – I had	ich habe – ich hatte
	I make – I made	ich mache – ich habe gemacht
	I come – I came	ich komme – ich kam
	I go – I went	ich gehe – ich bin gegangen
	I win – I won	ich gewinne – ich habe gewonnen
	I see – I saw	ich sehe – ich habe gesehen
	I find – I found	ich finde – ich habe gefunden
	I give – I gave	ich gebe – ich habe gegeben

Birthdays and parties

My birthday is in the **summer**.	spring • autumn • winter
I'm now **11**.	12 • 13
I had a party with my **friends**.	family
The party was on the **beach**.	at home • in a park
It started at **3** o'clock.	2 • 4 • 5
I made lots of food.	My mum • My dad • My grandma • My uncle
We ate **pizza**.	cake • hamburgers • sandwiches
We drank **water**.	lemonade • orange juice
We played **on the beach**.	in the garden • computer games • football
And we **listened to music**.	watched a film • went to the cinema
The party finished at **7** o'clock.	6 • 8 • 9
I had a **great** day.	good • fantastic
After the party I was **tired**!	happy

Write about a party. Schreib über eine Feier.

5 Unit

By the sea

The ferry

Cawsand Beach

1 Read the text. Lies den Text.

Cawsand Beach is near Plymouth. There are a lot of tourists at Cawsand Beach in the summer, but not in the winter. The tourists love the beach!

The Plymouth kids love Cawsand Beach too. They often take the ferry there from Plymouth. You can take the bus to Cawsand beach too. The ferry is nice on a warm day. You can see seals from the ferry. And you can see a lot of boats – blue boats, red boats, green boats, … The ferry takes 30 minutes.

Cawsand beach isn't big, but it's clean. The beach is great for kids, but you can't take dogs there. You can see seals on the rocks. You can go swimming and sailing or you can play ball games on the beach. You can have a picnic or you can go to a nice café or restaurant. And you can buy an ice cream at one of the small shops – yummy!

2 Right or wrong? Richtig oder falsch?

	Right	Wrong
1 Cawsand Beach is near London.	☐	☐
2 A lot of tourists go there in the winter.	☐	☐
3 The Plymouth kids often take the ferry to Cawsand Beach.	☐	☐
4 Cawsand Beach is big.	☐	☐
5 You can take dogs there.	☐	☐
6 Seals have picnics at Cawsand Beach.	☐	☐
7 There are nice cafés and shops there.	☐	☐
8 The ice cream is fantastic!	☐	☐

TIP
Deine Lernwörter findest du ab Seite 85.

3 Match the ticket prices and ferry times. Verbinde die Preise und Zeiten.

Ferry times

The ferry leaves every day at the following times:

From: Plymouth Beach	From: Cawsand
10:30	11:00
12:00	12:30
14:30	15:00
16:00	16:30

The trip takes 30 minutes.

Prices (one way per person)

Adult	£4
Child	£2

Babies and bikes are FREE!

10:30	ferry ticket for an adult
16:30	trip from Plymouth to Cawsand
30 minutes	first ferry to Cawsand
£4	ferry ticket for a baby or a bike
£2	last ferry to Plymouth
£0	ferry ticket for a child

4 Answer the questions. Beantworte die Fragen.

1 Nina and I want to go to Cawsand after lunch. What time is the ferry from Plymouth?

1 ______________

2 I want to go to Cawsand and take my bike. How much is it?

2 ______________

3 I want to go to Cawsand on Sunday. How long is the trip?

3 ______________

4 We want to go to Cawsand tomorrow. How much are the tickets?

4 ______________

Wenn du gerade etwas tust, sagst du das so: **I'm playing cards.**

5 Match the pictures and the sentences. Ordne die Bilder und Sätze zu.

6 What are you doing? Was machst du gerade?

I'm sitting in the classroom.

Ex. 6 und 9: Stärkere S können mehr Sätze schreiben.

Wenn du gerade etwas *nicht* tust, sagst du das so: **I'm not talking to a friend.**

7 Complete the table with the -ing form. Vervollständige die Tabelle.

play	I'm not playing	watch	______
read	______	write	______

8 Complete the sentences. Vervollständige die Sätze.

I'm not playing • I'm not reading • I'm not watching • ~~I'm not writing~~

1 I'm not writing ______ a story, Sam,
I'm writing the answers to the quiz!

2 ______ with Morph,
I'm playing with Silky.

3 ______ a video,
I'm on skype with a friend.

4 ______ the text message,
I'm looking at the photo.

9 And you? Write 3 sentences. Und du? Schreib 3 Sätze.

I'm not ______ German. I'm writing English.

______ in my bedroom. I'm sitting in the classroom.

______

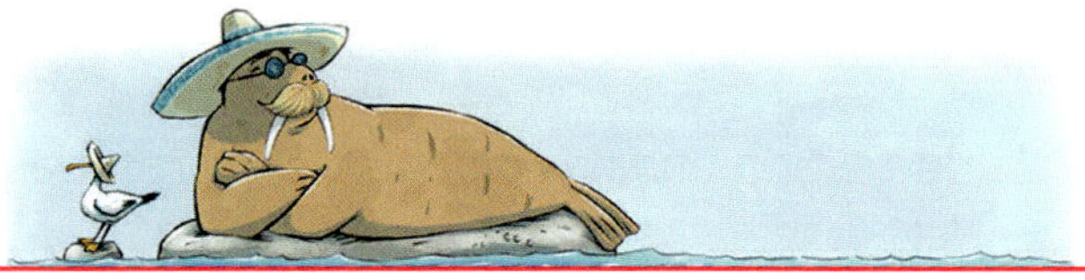

Wenn jemand gerade etwas tut, sagst du das so: Silky **is** swimming. The kids **are** swimming too.	Wenn jemand gerade etwas nicht tut, sagst du das so: Wilbur **isn't** swimming. Wilbur and the seagull **aren't** swimming.

10 Complete the sentences. Vervollständige die Sätze.

is eating • isn't eating • is playing • isn't playing • ~~is swimming~~ • ~~isn't swimming~~ • ~~are eating~~ • ~~aren't eating~~ • are running • aren't running • are watching • aren't watching

1 Amira is swimming ______________. She isn't swimming ______________ with Emily.

2 Charlie ______________ with the crabs. He ______________ with a ball.

3 Lily ______________ an ice cream. She ______________ a pizza.

4 Dan and his friend are eating ______________ sandwiches. They aren't eating ______________ crabs.

5 Two seagulls ______________ Dan and his friend. They're hungry!

They ______________ Lily.

6 Two boys ______________ after a ball.

They ______________ after the seagulls.

Wenn du wissen willst, **was** jemand tut, fragst du das so:

What is the boy doing?
– He**'s** singing.

What are the kids doing?
– They**'re** eating lunch.

Wenn du wissen willst, **wo** jemand etwas tut, fragst du das so:

Where is the boy singing?
– He**'s** singing in the Music Club.

Where are the kids eating lunch?
– They**'re** eating lunch in the canteen.

11 Match the text and the pictures. Ordne Text und Bilder zu.

What is the girl doing?
– She's texting a friend.

What is Sammy the dog doing?
– He's drinking water.

Where is the boy making cakes?
– He's making cakes in the kitchen.

Where are the boys playing football?
– They're playing football in the park.

12 Add the questions. Füge die Fragen ein.

Abby Tim, Mum is calling. She's shopping.

Tim I can't hear you. What is Mum doing?
Abby She's shopping at the Broadway.

Tim Sorry. Where ____________________?
Abby At the Broadway! And Dad is sailing with Uncle John.

Tim I can't hear you, Abby. What ____________________?
Abby He's sailing with Uncle John at Cawsand Beach.

Tim Sorry, I don't understand. ____________________
Abby Oh Tim! You aren't listening to me! AT CAWSAND BEACH!! And what are you doing?
Tim Me? I'm listening to you!

13 Answer the questions. Beantworte die Fragen.

Come to Plymouth Aquarium and see over 4 000 fish and other sea animals!

Opening times
Open every day 10 am – 6 pm

Prices

Adults	£11.75
Children 5-15 years	£ 7.75
Family tickets	£33.00

Café
Visit the Waves Café for a hot or cold drink, a snack, a cream tea or lunch.

How to find us
Take the No. 25 bus.
From the bus stop it's a 3-minute walk.

1 Was gibt es dort zu sehen?
2 Wie sind die Öffnungszeiten?
3 Was kostet der Eintritt pro Kind?
4 Mit welchem Bus kommen wir dahin?

14 Find pairs. Put them in the sentences. Finde Wortpaare. Füge sie ein.

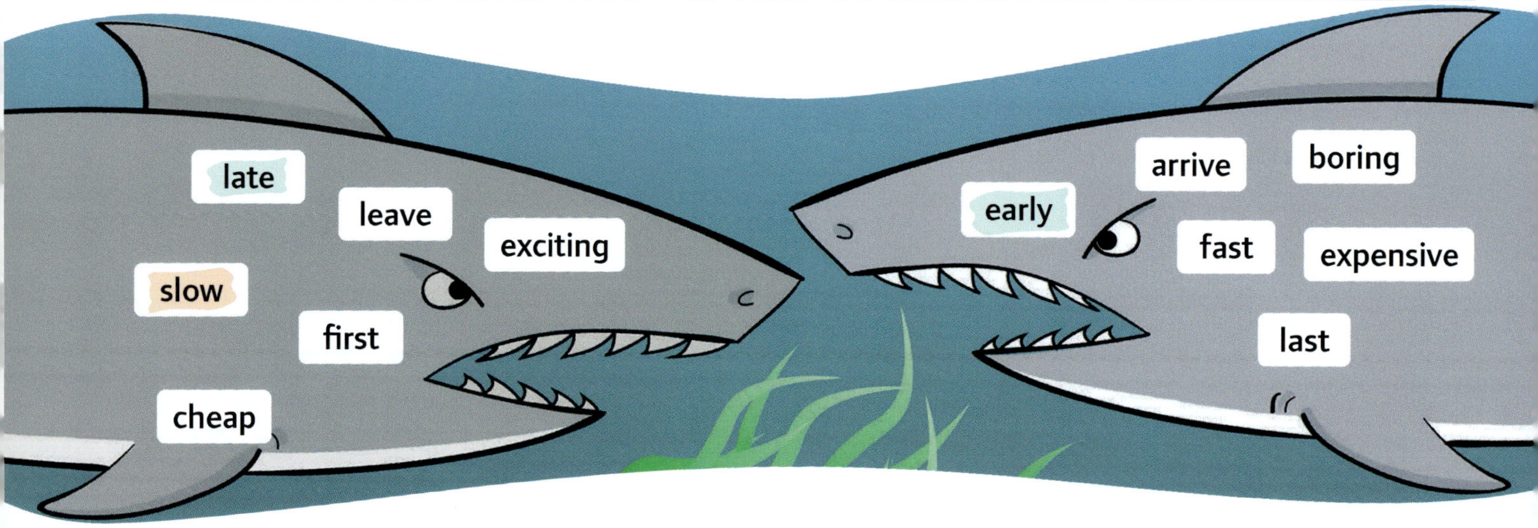

1 The ferry to Cawsand Beach is cheap ______ . It isn't ______ .

2 The ______ ferry to Cawsand is at 10:30 and the last ______ ferry back is at 16:30.

3 We leave ______ Plymouth at 10:30 and we ______ in Cawsand at 11:00.

4 Plymouth is great. It's an ______ city. It's not boring ______ .

5 The city tour is at 9:30. Don't be late ______ . Come ______ !

6 The Wheel isn't scary. The ride is ______ . It isn't fast ______ .

Ex. 13 ist als Mediation-Aufgabe gedacht. Deshalb können die Antworten auf Deutsch gegeben werden.
In Übung 14 zunächst sicherstellen, dass die Bedeutung der Wortpaare klar ist.

Auf Fragen mit *Can we …?* antwortest du so:

Can we go?
Yes, we can.

Can we go?
No, we can't.

15 Answer Noah's questions. Beantworte Noahs Fragen.

Can we play here?

____

Can we take the dog?

____

Can we buy ice cream here?

____

Can we swim here?

____

Can we play football here?

____

16 Fill in: *him, her, it* or *them*. Füge *him, her, it* oder *them* ein.

1 Where are the Plymouth kids? – I can see **them** on the beach.

2 Look, there is a seagull! Justin is filming ______________ .

3 Where is Sam? – Abby is playing chess with ______________ .

4 Maya has a good book. She's reading ______________ .

5 How many crabs can you see? Can you count ______________ ?

6 Can you see Silky? – Yes, I can see ______________ . She's sleeping on a rock!

Remember:
Where is Sam?
Can you see him?

Where is Lucy?
Can you see her?

Where is my book?
Can you see it?

Where are Maya and Justin?
Can you see them?

Where are my books?
Can you see them?

Ex. 16: Zur Unterstützung das Bild im SB auf S. 106 heranziehen.

17 Read the play. Lies das Theaterstück.

In the 18th century pepper was very expensive in England. It was much cheaper in France. This is a play about pepper smugglers in Cawsand.
Cook works in the kitchen at the Red Lion pub in Cawsand.
Molly works in the kitchen at the pub too. She's poor.
Flynn is Molly's brother. He's poor too.
Mr Collins is a bad man. He's very rich.
Tom, Jack and **Old Bill** were farmers. Now they're pepper smugglers.

The pepper smugglers

Scene 1: At the Red Lion

Molly and Cook are in the kitchen in the Red Lion pub in Cawsand.

Molly: Cook! Look! There are 3 smugglers in the dining room.
Cook: I know the 3 men, Molly. Tom, Jack and Old Bill.
Molly: But look – they have maps and plans. They're pepper smugglers. My brother Flynn wants to work with them!!

Cook: The 3 men are poor, Molly. They were farmers. Mr Collins took away their farms. He took away your parents' farm too. Now Mr Collins is rich and you, your brother and the 3 men are poor.

Flynn comes into the pub. He's very happy.
Flynn: Molly, I'm so happy. Soon I can buy you a new dress.
Molly: But I don't want a new dress. Flynn, you can't work with the pepper smugglers.
Flynn: Molly, Tom, Jack and Old Bill are my friends. We have a great plan. Please help me. We can be rich.
Cook: Molly, help your brother.

Molly and Flynn go out.

18th century 18. Jahrhundert · **pepper** Pfeffer · **expensive** teuer · **much cheaper** viel billiger · **farmers** Bauern · **maps** Landkarten · **took away** nahm weg · **parents** Eltern · **sell** verkaufen · **boxes of potatoes** Kisten mit Kartoffeln · **sword** Schwert · **throw** werfen

Scene 2: At Cawsand Beach

Cawsand Beach at night. Tom, Jack and Flynn are waiting for the ship with pepper.

Flynn: Look! I can see a man on the hill. I think it's Mr Collins.

Tom: Flynn, I can't see a man. Look! There's the ship from France with our pepper.

Jack: Come on, let's go!

The 3 men go to the ship in their boat. Soon they have the pepper.

Jack: We can sell the pepper at the market in Plymouth for a lot of money. But first let's take the pepper to Tom's house.

Scene 3: In Tom's kitchen

In Tom's kitchen. Molly and Flynn put the bags of pepper into boxes of potatoes.

Molly: Mr Collins was in the pub yesterday. He knows about your plans.

Flynn: Mr Collins can't stop us now.

Molly: He has a sword, Flynn. He's a bad man.

Tom: Come on, Flynn. It's time to take the potatoes to the market.

Flynn: Goodbye, Molly.

Scene 4: On Tom's boat

Tom's boat at Cawsand Beach. Molly is on the boat, but Tom and Flynn can't see her. Soon the boxes of potatoes (and pepper!) are on the boat.

Tom: Come on Flynn. Let's sail to the market in Plymouth.

Flynn: Oh no! Look! Mr Collins with his sword.

Mr Collins: I was on the hill. I know you have pepper in the boxes of potatoes. You're smugglers! Come out of the boat! Now!

Flynn: You can't stop us!

Mr Collins: Yes, I can.

Mr Collins is on the boat now. Molly throws potatoes onto the deck. Mr Collins falls. Then Molly throws pepper into Mr Collins' face.

Mr Collins: Help! Help!

Molly: Why? You took our farms.

Flynn takes the sword.

Flynn: Now leave the boat. What you can do with a sword, we can do with pepper!

Mr Collins is back on the beach. Tom, Flynn and Molly are very happy!

Flynn: To the market! Let's go to Plymouth.

16 Complete the sentences. Vervollständige die Sätze.

friends • ~~kitchen~~ • market • meet • Molly • money • Mr Collins • pepper smugglers • plan

Molly and Cook work in the kitchen ____________ at the pub.

Tom, Jack and Old Bill ____________ at the Red Lion pub.

Flynn meets his new ____________ at the pub.

They have a good ____________.

The men are ____________.

They want make a lot of ____________!

____________ knows about their plan.

He wants to stop the pepper smugglers, but ____________ helps the men.

The men take the pepper to the ____________ in Plymouth.

17 Who thinks what? Match. Wer denkt was? Ordne zu.

I'm too old to go in the boat with Tom, Jack and Flynn.

I hope Molly can help her brother.

- Cook
- man on the ship from France
- Old Bill
- Molly
- Mr Collins

I was right. The men are pepper smugglers.

I hope my brother is OK.

There is the boat from England.

S. 74	**At the beach**	**Am Strand**	
	tourist	Tourist	______
	take the ferry	die Fähre nehmen	______
	take the bus	den Bus nehmen	______
	go swimming	schwimmen gehen	______
	go sailing	segeln gehen	______
	play ball games	Ballspiele machen	______
	have a picnic	ein Picknick machen	______
	go to a café	in ein Café gehen	______
	go to a restaurant	in ein Restaurant gehen	______
	buy an ice cream	ein Eis kaufen	______

S. 76 f.	**doing things**	**etwas gerade tun**
	I'm writing a text	ich schreibe gerade eine SMS
	I'm playing football	ich spiele gerade Fußball
	I'm sitting in the classroom	ich sitze gerade im Klassenzimmer
	I'm listening to music	ich höre gerade Musik
	I'm doing my homework	ich mache gerade meine Hausaufgaben
	I'm phoning my friend	ich telefoniere gerade mit meiner Freundin
	I'm reading a book	ich lese gerade ein Buch
	I'm wearing my blue shoes	ich habe meine blauen Schuhe an
	I'm doing gymnastics	ich turne gerade
	I'm going to the library	ich gehe gerade in die Bücherei
	I'm cleaning my bedroom	ich putze gerade mein Zimmer
	I'm writing an email	ich schreibe gerade eine E-Mail

S. 77	**not doing things**	**etwas gerade nicht tun**
	I'm not doing my homework	ich mache gerade keine Hausaufgaben
	I'm not playing with my sister	ich spiele gerade nicht mit meiner Schwester
	I'm not reading	ich lese gerade nicht
	I'm not watching TV	ich gucke gerade nicht fern
	I'm not writing an email	ich schreibe gerade keine E-Mail

S. 80	**Opposites**	**Gegensätze**	
	early – late	früh – spät	______________
	leave – arrive	abfahren – ankommen	______________
	slow – fast	langsam – schnell	______________
	exciting – boring	aufregend – langweilig	______________
	good – bad	gut – schlecht	______________
	first – last	erster – letzter	______________
	cheap – expensive	billig – teuer	______________

S. 81	**Pronouns**	**Pronomen**
	him Can you see Sam? Can you see him?	ihn Kannst du Sam sehen? Kannst du ihn sehen?
	her Can you see Lucy? Can you see her?	sie Kannst du Lucy sehen? Kannst du sie sehen?
	it Can you see my phone? Can you see it?	es Kannst du mein Telefon sehen? Kannst du es sehen?
	Tim + Abbey = them Can you see Tim and Abby? Can you see them?	sie Kannst du Tim und Abby sehen? Kannst du sie sehen?
	the signs = them Can you read the signs? Can you read them?	sie Kannst du die Schilder lesen? Kannst du sie lesen?

Asking questions. Fragen stellen.

Du willst herausfinden, wann der Bus fährt:
What time is the bus?

Du willst herausfinden, wie teuer etwas ist:
How much is it?

Du willst herausfinden, was jemand gerade macht:
What are you doing?
What is Dan doing?
What are Lucy and Maya doing?

Du willst herausfinden, wo jemand gerade hingeht:
Where are you going?
Where is Abby going?
Where are Sam and Justin going?

Du willst herausfinden, ob man irgendwo spielen kann:
Can we play here?

Du willst herausfinden, ob man irgendwo Eis kaufen kann:
Can we buy ice cream here?

A holiday message

Hello, (name of your friend),	Hi
I'm in (name of place).	We're
I'm having a **good** holiday.	great · fantastic
The weather is **fantastic**.	good · great · bad
It's **very hot**.	warm · hot · cold
I **go swimming** every day.	play games · meet my friends
The food is **yummy**.	OK · great
See you **after the holidays**.	soon · next week

Bye!
(your name)

1 How old is Silky? [p. 2]

- ☐ 2
- ☐ 3

2 What day comes after Wednesday? [p. 4]

- ☐ Monday
- ☐ Tuesday
- ☐ Thursday

3 Who is not at Plymstock School? [p. 14]

- ☐ Lucy
- ☐ Abby
- ☐ Maya

4 Who has a dog – Charlie? [p. 18]

- ☐ Abby
- ☐ Dan

5 Who has a little sister? [p. 22]

- ☐ Sam
- ☐ Lucy
- ☐ Justin

6 What does Justin have? [p. 38]

- ☐ a video camera
- ☐ a new phone
- ☐ a dog

7 Does Morph like cats? [p. 48]

- ☐ Yes, he does.
- ☐ No, he doesn't.

8 Where does Justin's dad live? [p. 52]

- ☐ in New York
- ☐ in Boston
- ☐ in Chicago

9 What does Justin want to film? [p. 56]

- ☐ Lucy's dream
- ☐ Abby's dream
- ☐ Sam's dream

10 Where was Dan's party? [p. 63]

- ☐ in his garden
- ☐ in the park
- ☐ at the beach

11 Was Abby at Lucy's birthday party? [p. 66]

- ☐ Yes, she was.
- ☐ No, she wasn't.

12 What did Abby give Silky? [p. 68]

- ☐ her name
- ☐ some milk
- ☐ a new home

13 Can you take dogs to Cawsand Beach? [p. 74]

- ☐ Yes, you can.
- ☐ No, you can't.

14 What did the smugglers want to sell? [p. 83]

- ☐ gold
- ☐ potatoes
- ☐ pepper